Rachel P. Lamberson
Realtor

Bus: (909) 294-2393
E-mail: steraclam@aol.com
Web: www.rplamberson.com

I am pleased to present you with "Temecula Wine Country: The Undiscovered Jewel of Southern California." This book is offered to help acquaint you with Southern California's beautiful wine region, it's lovely rolling landscapes, lively history and award winning wineries. May this book serve as a memento of Temecula, California and my appreciation for your continued business and referrals.

Century 21
Wright

D0001646

TEMECULA WINE COUNTRY

The Undiscovered Jewel of Southern California

WRITTEN BY
Gia Danson-Lucy

PHOTOGRAPHS BY
Peter Phan and Gia Danson-Lucy

VISTA PACIFICA PUBLISHING COMPANY
Dana Point, California

Credits

First published in the United States in 2003
by Vista Pacifica Publishing Company
P.O. Box 373
Dana Point, CA 92629
(949) 395-2878
www.vistapacificapublishing.com

Library of Congress Control Number: 2003102113
ISBN: 0-9679452-1-6
First Edition
Printed in China

Designer: Robert Brocke
Editor: Richard J. Collins
Proof Reader: Theresa Moos
Photography: Gia Danson-Lucy, Peter Phan
Photo Stylist: Karen Lucy
Foreword by: Cane Vanderhoof- Miramonte Winery

Although the author and publisher has made every effort to ensure
the accuracy of the information contained in this book, we assume no
responsibility for errors, inaccuracies, omissions, or any inconsistency
herein. Further, we assume no liability for any loss, injury, or inconvenience
sustained by any traveler as a result of information or advice contained
in *Temecula Wine County: The Undiscovered Jewel Of Southern California*.

To my family, thank you for always celebrating in my joy and supporting me in all that I do. I love you.

To Peter Phan, my dear friend and talented photographer, your stunning photographs have made this book beautiful. Thank you.

To Robert Brocke, once again your creative talents and hard work have produced a stunning piece of work. You are truly invaluable.

To Karen Lucy, thank you for spending countless hours in the backyard composing photo scenes.

To Richard Collins, my grandfather and true friend, thank you for your guidance and encouragement. You are wonderful.

Additionally, I would like to acknowledge The Grapeline Wine Country Shuttle and Temecula Wine County's estate owners for so graciously sponsoring the book with complimentary tours and wine tasting and sharing stories and information about their winery.

"The Lord's loving kindnesses indeed never cease, For His compassions never fail.
They are new every morning; Great is Thy faithfulness." – *Lamentations 3:22-23*

Table of Contents

TEMECULA WINE COUNTRY

Los Angeles

San Bernardino

Riverside

Anaheim

Corona

Palm Springs

Long Beach

Irvine

Lake Elsinore

Hemet
Idyllwild

Temecula

San Clemente

Oceanside

Carlsbad

Escondido

Del Mar

San Diego

N

W ● E

S

Los Angeles
90 miles

15

215

79

Winchester Road

Jefferson Avenue

Ynez Road

Front Street

Old Town Temecula

Rancho

California Road

Margarita Road

Ynez Road

Butterfield Stage Road

Pauba Road

La Serena

Calle Contento

Anza Road

Pauba Road

De Portola Road

Monte de Oro Rd.

Glenoaks Road

Barnsdale Circle

Wilson Creek

Longshadow Ranch

Mount Palomar

Miramonte

Baily

Faulkner

Ponte

Palumbo

South Coast

Van Roekel

Maurice Car'rie

Callaway Coastal

Hart

Churon

Stuart Cellars

Cilurzo

Filsinger

Thornton

Keyways

15

79

San Diego
60 miles

9

Temecula wine country is abuzz with energy, the inexplicable energy of creation that gives way to mankind's desire to shape and change things, to turn nothing into something – something tangible, something of pride, something of elegance, distinction and sophistication. Yes, Temecula is abuzz with an extraordinarily creative winemaking spirit.

And why not? It's about time. A generation ago, a colorful group of pioneering enophiles saw the possibilities of this region to grow grapes of exquisite quality. And it has taken every bit of that generation, and even part of a second, to learn exactly what grapes to grow, where to grow them, and how to grow them properly within our appellation's many microclimates. But now we know. And now we're consistently creating approachable, well-crafted wines that show the degree of complexity one looks for in the best wines of the world. Indeed, in one wine competition after another, we continue to receive numerous awards and medals for our latest creations. Even better, the public at large is recognizing our craftsmanship, as we continue to interpret traditional wine varietals in ways that surprise and thrill them.

And so, Temecula Wine Country has arrived. Most of our wineries are family owned and operated, the way wineries probably should be. But our winemaking adolescence as an appellation is over, and now is our time to shine.

This feeling is infectious. At the time of this writing, several new wineries have either been built, or are currently under construction.

So, I commend Gia Lucy on recognizing the forces of change currently at work in Temecula, and I commend her desire to share these changes with you. This book is written and photographed with the same passion with which we Temecula winemakers craft our wines. It is written with the hope that it might prompt you to come share the discovery of our appellation.

The sun, the rain, the soil, the vine - these are the tools with which we vintners create. I invite you to come experience for yourself just what it is we are creating with them, here in Temecula Wine Country.

Cheers,

Cane Vanderhoof – Miramonte Winery

Temecula's Wine Country is sometimes called Southern California's Napa Valley. And although the climate, wine, estates and landscape mirror that of California's northern wine region, the Temecula Valley is altogether different.

I was first introduced to Temecula a year ago by Ray Falkner, the owner of Falkner Winery. We had met in my hometown of San Clemente at a wine tasting event, and he had invited me to visit his family's estate. I was fascinated by his descriptions of the town, countryside, wineries and the numerous events they offered. But what intrigued me most was the quality and variety of the wine made in the valley.

The drive to Temecula along Highway 76 was just as charming as Ray had promised. The pretty two-lane highway took me past fresh fruit stands, along grassy meadows, and through hills covered in orchids, then veered north to meet Interstate -15, which leads into the valley.

The moment I arrived, I was immediately delighted by the layout of the town and its storybook perfect setting. The fact that almost all of the wineries are built along one very long road, Rancho California, which is fetchingly lined with verdant rolling vineyards and grand estates, makes it easy to visit and taste the wines at all the different wineries. It surprised me to discover that unlike Napa and Sonoma, Temecula was not well known for its wine region. My desire to share this hidden treasure inspired me to write this book.

One month later I was back on that same road, this time with photographer, Peter Phan, returning to capture the landscapes, people, wines, history, and estates, of Temecula Wine Country - The Undiscovered Jewel Of Southern California.

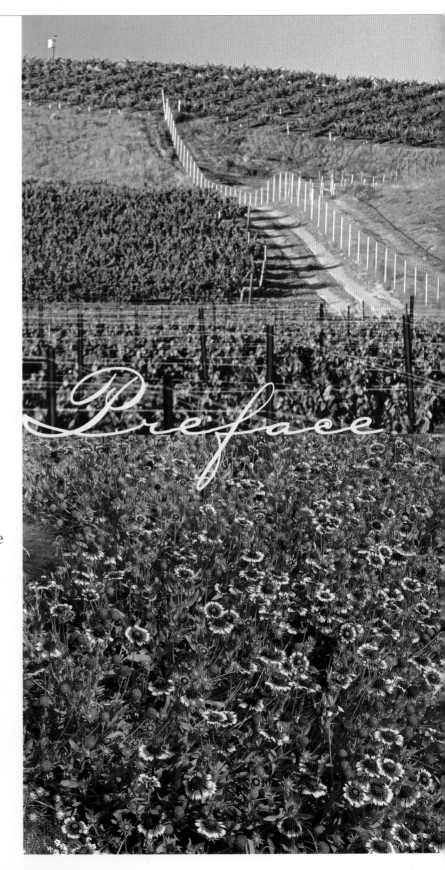

Two hundred years ago, Father Juan Norberto de Santiago – a Spanish Missionary from Mission San Juan Capistrano – and his exploring party of seven soldiers descended upon what is now the Temecula Valley, searching for a site to build a new mission. What they discovered was a tribe of Indians living in a lush valley with rolling hills, rich soil and a mild climate. Twenty-four years later in 1821, the Mission San Luis Rey began to Christianize the local residents and took control over this region, cultivating the land. This area proved to be a golden Eden and reaped a bounty of grain crops for the mission.

Today it's the variety of fertile vineyards and award winning wineries lying within easy reach of one another that makes this region irresistible. In the past decade, wines made here have garnered much attention and many awards. They are as diverse as California's climate and geography, and are unique in this part of California, partially due to the Rainbow Gap – an opening in the coastal mountains that funnels cool maritime breezes from the Pacific Ocean some twenty miles away, and results in a warm dry climate ideal for growing grapes. During the evening and into the morning the valley settles under a heavy sea mist, which lifts by mid-day to reveal brilliant sunshine, spilling across the vineyards.

Temecula

Valley

16

The city itself is laid out as two distinct halves: Old Town to the east and Rancho California to the west. Old Town has a character and architecture defined by its history as a western town. From the mid 1840's through the mid 1960's, Temecula's economy centered around cattle and agriculture. It was a land whose very name promised adventure and excitement. There were rancheros and vaqueros, Indians, gold miners, general stores, saloons and famous stagecoach and bank robberies. Over the years, this "trading post for the residents of Temecula Valley" turned into a "dwindling handful of wind-worn, dusty buildings" (*California: American Guide Series, December 1946*.) Today, Old Town Temecula has been restored and looks like a scene from some marvelous children's book of western tales with a wooden boardwalk and picturesquely clustered western storefronts which have been converted into antique shops, boutiques and restaurants. Many of the original buildings have been designated historical sites and can be seen on a walking tour of the town.

Once outside Old Town, the scenery changes abruptly from a Wild West atmosphere to a stretch of chain restaurants and residential housing communities. But continue along Rancho California Road and soon the fragrant scent of orange blossoms, carried on the warm ocean breeze, delights your senses and Wine Country comes into view. Presently, there are eighteen wineries throughout the valley and more on the way. Each estate is unique in terms of architecture, atmosphere and varietals; and all offer wine tasting. So raise your glass and toast Temecula Wine Country - The Undiscovered Jewel Of Southern California.

17

Wine Country

Thornton Winery

There are several reasons why visitors love Thornton Winery and make a positive effort to include it in their tours of Temecula – one being Thornton's sparkling California champagne, produced in the traditional fashion of the Methode Champenoise. Other enticements include delicious gourmet meals served al fresco on a lovely terrace overlooking rolling vineyards, and critically acclaimed contemporary jazz concerts performed on the Mediterranean fountain terrace.

Thornton also produces classic still wines modeled after the Mediterranean and Rhone regions. Guests can take pleasure in wine tasting indoors or on a shaded patio at the winery's Champagne Lounge, or enjoy formal dining and contemporary fusion cuisine delightfully paired with wine at the award winning four-star Café Champagne.

Perhaps the best time to visit Thornton Winery is on Sunday afternoons, spring through fall, during The Champagne Jazz concert series, which features nationally renowned jazz artists. This intimate venue affords good views for the entire audience with concert-style seating as well as tables where guests can enjoy dinner while watching the show.

The winery comes to life the moment the musicians step on stage. The audience cheers as the music starts and many guests saunter to the dance floor where they continue the tradition of whirling cloth napkins above their head as they bend and sway to the music.

EVENTS

Thornton Winery's best-known event, The Champagne Jazz Concert Series, provides first-rate entertainment spring through fall. Throughout the year, the winery continues its reputation for fine entertainment with Winemaker Dinners, Halloween Murder Mystery Nights, a New Year's Eve black-tie gala, cooking classes and wedding facilities.

CHAMPAGNE LIST

Natural
Brut Reserve
Cuvee de Frontignan
Cuvee Rouge
NV Brut
Blanc de Noir

CHAMPAGNE MUST TASTE

Cuvee Rouge

WINE LIST

Chardonnay
Pinot Blanc
Viognier
Sauvignon Blanc
Moscato Grenache Rose
Cabernet-Merlot
Cabernet Sauvignon
Aleatico
Old Vine Zinfandel
Syrah
Cote Red
Sangiovese

MUST TASTE

Cote Red

23

In recent years, many Southern California wine lovers have discovered the small but delightful wine region of the Temecula Valley. Long overshadowed by the well known and popular Napa and Sonoma wine areas, Temecula is now coming into its own and garnering the attention and awards worthy of a fine wine country destination.

On any given afternoon, visitors from all over Southern California enjoy picnicking and wine tasting at the many estates situated along Rancho California Road and adjacent drives. Often, they discover that a one-day visit is not sufficient to take advantage of all this area has to offer and decide it might be desirable to stay overnight, perhaps at the French-styled Inn at Churon.

CHURON WINERY

Churon is the first Bed & Breakfast winery combination in Southern California. It is aesthetically stunning with large picture windows, lush vineyards and a lovely garden with a latticed gazebo. The lobby is equally as grand, boasting a thirty-five foot ceiling with murals of hot air balloons lofting over vineyards and handsome paintings from the winery's monthly revolving artist show.

Check in early and begin your day by visiting Temecula's various estates, purchase cheese and a bottle of wine and relax under the shade of an oak tree, then return to the inn for a guests-only wine tasting.

At the end of the evening sink into the comfortable four-poster bed with goose-down pillows and white linens, flip on the gas-burning fire place and dream of tomorrow – sailing above the still-darkened vineyards in a hot air balloon and watching the sun rise over the mountains instantly turning everything golden and warm.

WINE LIST

Viognier
Chardonnay
Syrah
Merlot
Cabernet Sauvignon
Muscat Canelli

MUST TASTE

Syrah

EVENTS

Churon's lovely grounds are ideal for weddings and banquets. The winery also features a romantic Valentine's dinner and New Year's Eve Galla.

27

Stuart Cellars

S tuart Cellars Winery is known for two things: a warm, welcoming atmosphere and premium crafted wines. Throughout the week visitors pour into Stuart Cellar's tasting room, lured by the lively selection of wines, which are prepared in a way that enhances the grapes natural flavors and reflects the winemaking traditions of the Old World. Upon entering the winery, guests are greeted with a quick and friendly smile and instantly feel part of the Stuart family.

Marshal and Susan Stuart opened Stuart Cellars in 1998 with the goal of making quality wines, which they could proudly share with friends and family. To that end, Marshal Stuart has never stopped short of his dream. His passion for wine has led him to take his job as owner and winemaker most seriously.

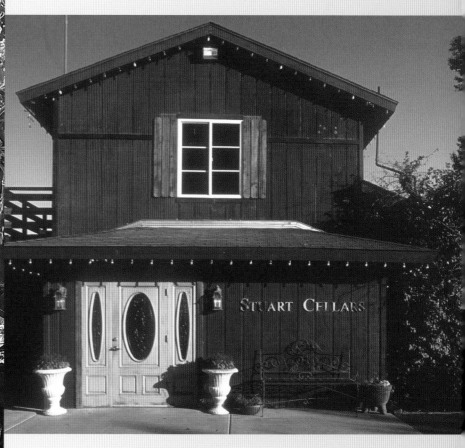

He plants his vineyards in the French tradition of north to south, which allows the grapes to ripen evenly on both sides of the vine, giving consistency to the fruit as well as providing protection from the sun's mid-day heat. He carefully thins the vines to concentrate more color and taste into each individual grape, which in turn intensifies the fruit's natural flavors and aromas. During Harvest, he places the fruit in small bins, rather than large ones, to prevent inadvertently crushing and damaging the yield, and then employs a cool fermentation process to pull the fruitiness from the grapes. Finally, he ages the wine in either American or French Oak barrels to impart the specific qualities and characteristics befitting the particular style of wine produced.

A wonderful way to end your day at Stuart Cellars is to purchase a bottle of estate wine and enjoy it at the winery's picnic area, which over-looks the Temecula Valley.

WINE LIST

Chardonnay
Viognier
Callista **(Blend of Chardonnay, Viognier, White Merlot, and Sauvignon Blanc)**
Pinot Noir
Sangiovese
Tatria **(Blend of Cabernet Sauvignon, Cabernet Franc, and Merlot)**
Cabernet Franc
Zinfandel
Merlot
Zinfandel Vintage Port

MUST TASTE

Pinot Noir

EVENTS

Stuart Cellars combines wine tasting with live music to create *Jazz at* Twilight Concerts on the Green, where guests enjoy dancing, dining and drinking, all under the stars. The winery also hosts barrel tastings and private parties.

31

Cilurzo Vineyards

When Vincenzo and Audrey Cilurzo first purchased 100 acres of land back in 1967, it was a different Temecula Valley than it is today. In those days it was a land of simple, uncluttered beauty, of rancheros and cattle, big skies, unpaved roads, and one stop sign erected simply to protect the ducks as they crossed the road. Upon entering the valley the signpost read, Population 350.

Vince Cilurzo was working as a senior lighting director for ABC in Los Angles in 1967 when he came across an article in the *Wall Street Journal* advertising agricultural land in Temecula, California. He decided to invest. He liked the promise of opportunity as well as a place to escape the hustle and bustle of his busy job.

Originally, he and his wife planned on growing avocados, but to their good fortune they met Dick Break, researcher for the University of California Davis. Break, who was surveying the valley for agricultural uses, discovered that the valley's climate was strikingly similar to that of the well-known Napa Valley wine region. So while almost everyone else in the valley was planting citrus groves, the Cilurzos went to Napa, purchased cuttings, and planted the very first vineyard in Temecula under the supervision of Dick Break.

33

Within four years, they were selling their grapes to local vineyards. In 1978 they decided to keep the best juice for themselves, and opened a winery that now produces some of the finest wines in the valley.

Today, the winery probably looks much like it did back in 1978: A modest brown building with hand painted signs directing guests up the drive to the winery entrance. But don't let this deter you. The interior of the building and the quality of their wine is far more interesting than the humble exterior suggests. One wall displays black and white pictures of rural Temecula in the1960's as well as framed photographs chronicaling Cilurzo's life as an Emmy- award winning senior lighting director for ABC. Many of the photographs include Cilurzo with American stars such as Brook Shields, Raquel Welch, Frank Sinatra and David Letterman.

WINE LIST

Chardonnay
Viognier
Sauvignon Blanc
Chenin Blanc
Zinfandel Rosé
Vincheno
Bordeaux Blend
Merlot
Petite Sirah
Muscat Canelli
Late Harvest Petite Sirah

MUST TASTE

Late Harvest Petite Sirah

EVENTS

The Cilurzo's extend their
hospitality to guests at an
annual Wine and Cigar
dinner, held at the owners'
home. A local chef prepares
a tantelizing dinner, which
guests enjoy on the outdoor
terrace overlooking the
estate's vineyards.

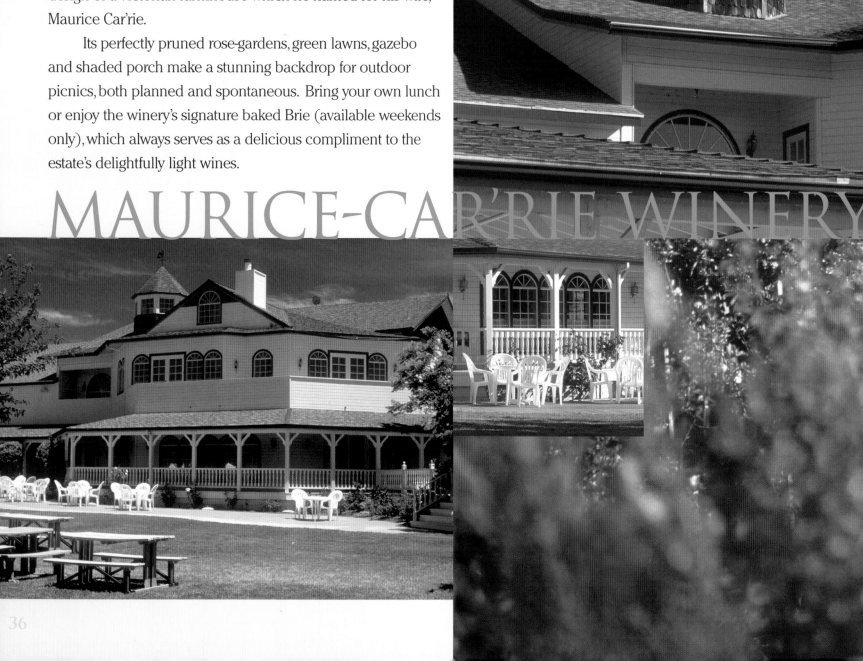

When Budd and Maurice Van Roekel bought a home with citrus groves in the Temecula Valley in 1984, they only wanted to take up a gracious life of retirement after a freeway expansion forced the sale of their Orange County roller skating rink of thirty-three years. For Bud, tending his orchids became a daily activity, then a passion that extended to the vineyards. In 1985 he bought 46-acres of vines, and a few years later built a winery in the architectural design of a Victorian farmhouse which he named for his wife, Maurice Car'rie.

Its perfectly pruned rose-gardens, green lawns, gazebo and shaded porch make a stunning backdrop for outdoor picnics, both planned and spontaneous. Bring your own lunch or enjoy the winery's signature baked Brie (available weekends only), which always serves as a delicious compliment to the estate's delightfully light wines.

MAURICE-CAR'RIE WINERY

Maurice Car'rie's winemaker, Mike Tingley, a rock-musician-turned-winemaker – who traded life on the road for a home in the valley with his family – now uses his artistic and scientific talents in creating a variety of approachable wines for inexperienced wine drinkers. (He is also the wine maker for Bud and Maurice's other winery, Van Roekel, which caters to sophisticated wine connoisseurs.) When asked if he misses performing music, he responds whimsically, "Winemaking suits my artistic side. Since I never know what Mother Nature is going to hand me, I must approach winemaking differently each year. That's what makes it so exciting. That's the love that all winemakers share."

WINE LIST

Private Reserve Chardonnay
Chardonnay
Sauvignon Blanc
Chenin Blanc Soft
Heather's Mist
Johannisberg Riesling
Cream Sherry
Muscat Canelli
Summer's End **(Sweet Dessert Wine)**
Sera Bella **(Fruity Blush-White Merlot)**
Cabernet Franc Rosé
White Zinfandel
Collage **(Premium Blended Red Wine)**
Merlot
Cabernet Sauvignon
Petite Sirah
Pinot Noir
Cody's Crush
(Blend of White & Red Wines)

CHAMPAGNE LIST

Maurice Car'rie Champagne

MUST TASTE

Sera Bella

EVENTS

Art and craft fairs are held each weekend on the front lawn at Maurice Car'rie Winery. Beneath the billowing white canopies, guests can find anything from fine gifts to artistic renderings of the valley.

39

VAN ROEKEL VINEYARDS &

WINERY

A handsome Dutch windmill set amongst colorful seasonal flowers beckons visitors up the short drive to hilltop Van Roekel Vineyard and Winery. This rather quaint site combines the charm and ambiance of old-world Holland with the inviting feel of grandmother's backyard. It is a delightful and must see stop along the Temecula wine tasting tour.

When Bud and Maurice Van Roekel purchased the sixty-acre winery and vineyards directly adjacent to their property, Maurice Car'rie Winery, in 1989, they only used the building as an oak barrel aging room and storage for addition stainless tanks.

Then in 1994 they had a novel idea. Why not cater to the entire wine drinking community by featuring wines created expressly for novice drinkers at Maurice Car'rie and premium wines crafted exclusively for wine connoisseurs at Van Roekel? Their inspiration is a hit!

Van Roekel's tasting room, a trim and tidy red brick building with green and white stitching, features seventeen premium wines. The extensive wine list runs the gamut from a gold medal Gewürztraminer to Syrah to dessert wine and champagne. Many of their wines have garnered awards, thanks in large part to the tireless efforts and extraordinary talents of Bud Van Roekel and Mike Tingley, the estate's vintner and winemaker respectively. Their passion for wine is certainly apparent and comes across in the quality of their wines.

WINE LIST

Pinot Gris
Chardonnay Aboire
Viognier
Chardonnay
Gewürztraminer
Fume Blanc
Rosé of Syrah
White Zinfandel
Merlot
Syrah
Grenache
Zinfandel
K Syrah Sirah
Cabernet Sauvignon
Allegria **(Dessert Wine)**
Sweet Salud **(Dessert Wine)**
Muscat of Alexandria **(Dessert Wine)**
Van Roekel Champagne

MUST TASTE

Grenache

The scenic drive along De Portola Road to Keyways Vineyard and Winery is so picturesque that visitors often become enamored of this winery before even reaching its doors. The five-mile drive from Rancho California Road takes you past grand estates where horses and cattle graze in the pastures and sunlight dances along the tops of the trees. Upon arrival at the winery, the setting is even more engaging: stately peppertrees cast shade onto a Spanish styled villa with red tile roofing, equestrian hitching posts and a long, lovely covered terrace where hanging flowerpots spill over with fragrant pink geraniums. Picnic tables and a close-by equestrian area are also available on the grounds for guests to enjoy.

KEYWAYS
VINEYARDS & WINERY

Many visitors are especially fond of the winery's tasting room that has the feel and character of an antique collector's attic. The room is filled with the most extraordinary collection of stuff: old gas lanterns, restored antique radios, a pot bellied stove, antique winemaking machinery and an electric train that chugs along on tracks positioned overhead. These items have no actual use; they are just lively, rather charming accessories. The tasting counter itself is a quaint old-fashioned copper topped bar which, in its prime, was used in an Old Town Temecula saloon.

WINE LIST

Chardonnay
Viognier
Cabernet Franc Estate
Cabernet Sauvignon
Merlot
Petite Syrah
Riesling
Late Harvest Zinfandel
Misty Key **(Blend of Riesling and Sauvignon Blanc)**

MUST TASTE

Late Harvest Zinfandel

EVENTS

Keyway Winery's rural location and picturesque setting make it an ideal travel destination for equestrian groups. Complete with hitching posts and corrals, riders can safely leave their horses and go inside to enjoy a bottle of wine.

47

Bilsinger Vineyards

F ilsinger Vineyards is a small, intimate winery situated along a quiet country road in the Temecula Valley. It has the allure of a working vineyard with a sense of tradition, few crowds, and an air that gives its visitors the feeling that they have discovered something unique. Guests feel as if they have in some way been transformed from simply a sightseer into someone who is now in the know.

Bill Filsinger, fondly known as "Doc" by many of Temecula's vintners (he practiced medicine in Orange County for thirty five years) is like many of the world's top winemakers – he is a farmer, more likely and much happier to be out in the vineyards or in the lab than any other place. He began planting his estate in 1978, diligently driving from Orange County each weekend to work in his fields and open the winery.

It wasn't difficult for Filsinger to give up his weekends. Wine making runs in his blood. His extended family were producers of wine, and at one time owned and operated a sizable winery in Mainz, Germany. Unfortunately, during World War II, Hitler's army confiscated their estate; and since it was impossible to return the winery to its previous success, they never reopened the winery.

Fortunately, Bill Filsinger brings the tradition and the name of his relatives to the Temecula Valley, producing the first Gewürztraminer in Southern California, many of the classic wines of the region, and California Champagne produced by the Méthode Champenoise.

WINE LIST
Chardonnay
Fumé Blanc
Gewürztraminer
Riesling
Grenache Blush
Zinfandel Rose
Orange Muscat
Black Muscat
Nebbiolo
Merlot
Cabernet Sauvignon
Grenache
Late Harvest Zinfandel

CHAMPAGNE LIST
Diamond Cuvee
Brut Rose

MUST TASTE
Gewürztraminer

This is a quaint out of the way, boutique winery whose specialty is red Mediterranean-style varietals. Although the tasting room is small, it is adequate and the large veranda showcases magnificent views of the local mountain range, giving visitors the feeling of being on vacation - far removed the cares of everyday life.

Perhaps this identical feeling is what prompted Nicholas Palumbo to purchase this property in 1998, on his very first visit to Temecula. In less than thirty days, he moved inland from his hometown of San Diego to the valley, where he revived his family's tradition of farming.

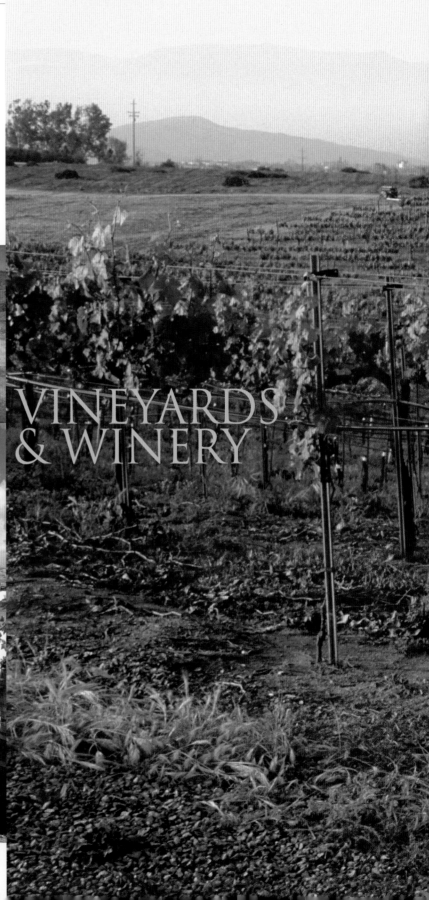

PALUMBO FAMILY VINEYARDS & WINERY

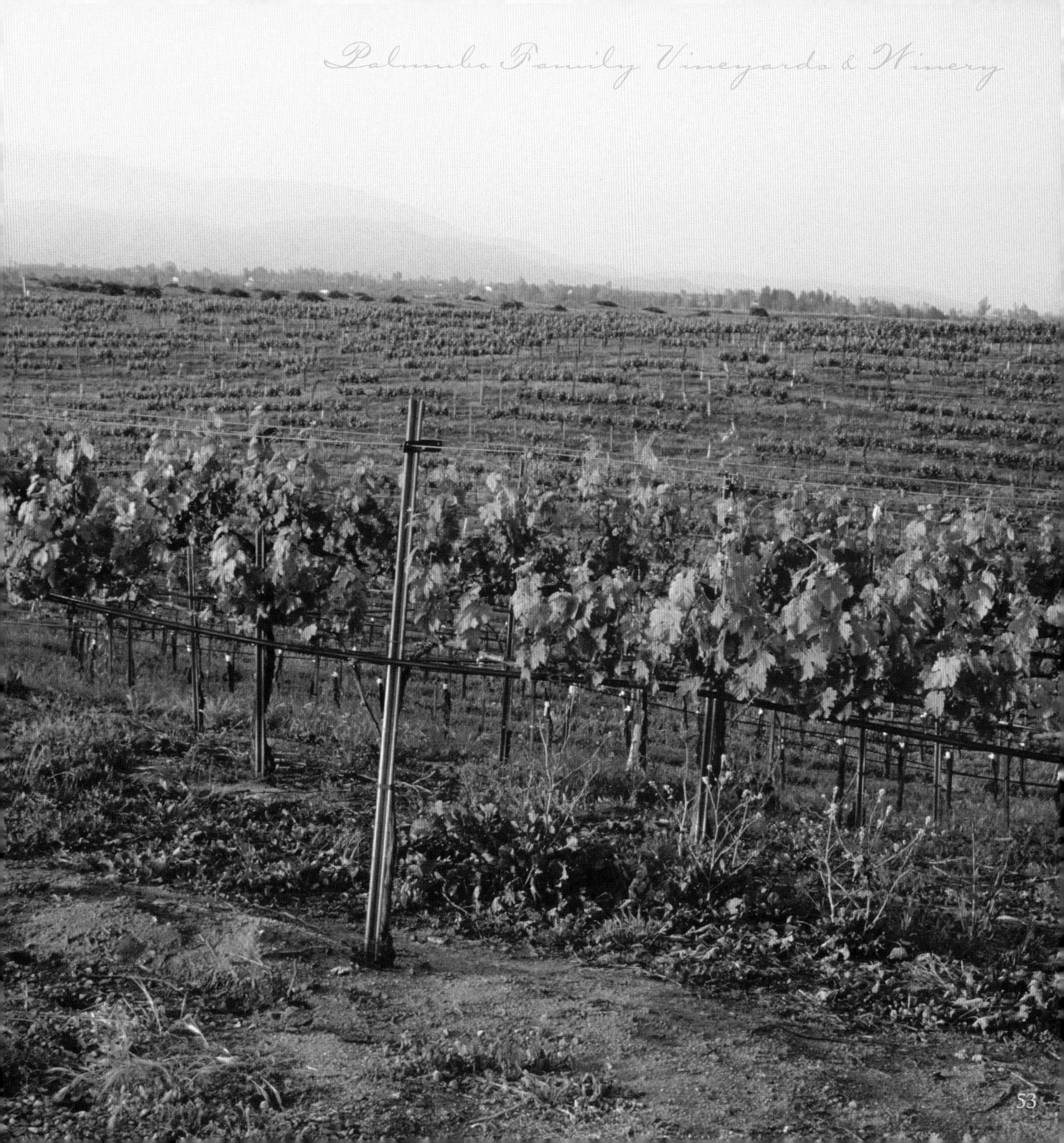

The first five years he sold his grapes to local wine makers – who often argued fiercely about which one would purchase Palumbo's Cabernet Franc grapes. Finally, in 2002, Nicholas Palumbo settled this debate by deciding not to sell. Instead, he opened his very own Palumbo Family Vineyards and Winery.

Similar to many renowned winemakers, Nicholas Palumbo believes that the best wines begin in the vineyard. This is why he insists on producing wines solely from the grapes he grows himself – it is his way of ensuring the high standards of excellence upon which his wines and reputation are built.

The winery, open Saturday and Sunday and by appointment during the week, also offers barbecues and private dinners from two to twelve people.

WINE LIST

Cabernet Franc
Cabernet Sauvignon
Late Harvest Merlot
Sangiovese

MUST TASTE

Cabernet Franc

Ponte Family Estate

J ohn Harrington in *The Englishman's Doctor*, 1968 writes:
"Five qualities there are wines praise advancing:
Strong, beautiful, fragrant, cool, and dancing."
The Ponte Family Estate Winery in Temecula exemplifies
this belief and shares with its visitors in the celebration of wine.
Conceived and built by two brothers, Claudio and Roberto
Ponte, grape growers in the area since 1984 the estate is
designed to leave visitors rejuvenated after spending a day in
the Temecula Wine Country. As the largest independent vineyard in the area with 450 acres of wine grapes the winery and
grounds are stunning.

35053

From the open beam ceilings in the tasting room "barn", to the handsome old mission serving as a cellar and barrel room, to the masterful gardens, every detail is brilliantly thought out and executed. Even the colors of the buildings reflect the vibrant hues of the vineyard.

The estate's Smokehouse Café is ideal for enjoying California Cuisine cleverly paired with a glass of estate wine. Chose from enjoying your meal picnic style on the lawns or dine on the veranda underneath a covered trellis, where misters keep you cool in the summer and heaters keep you warm in the winter. The vista from both venues rewards visitors with a view of pastoral splendor. For as far as the eye can see, row upon row of rolling grapevines stretches toward the mountains. This serene setting at Ponte Estate beckons visitors to stay.

WINE LIST

Cabernet
Merlot
Sauvignon Blanc
Chardonnay
Zinfandel Port
Isabel
Juliet
Belmonte Reserve
Nebbiola
Sangiovese
Barbera

MUST TASTE

Sauvignon Blanc

EVENTS

Surrounded by 350 acres of vineyards, Ponte makes an nice setting for weddings and special events. They also feature tours, winemaker dinners, cooking classes and a New Year's Eve gala.

Founded and operated by three generations of Wilsons, this winery has a cheerful, inviting air. The owners, Gerry and Rosie, refer to their visitors as "extended family" and go as far as sharing their prized recipes, which have been passed down from generation to generation. This warm and welcoming atmosphere has contributed to making Wilson Creek a favorite among many Southern California families.

WILSON CREEK WINERY

The Wilsons who have always been passionate about wine making – some thirty years ago they were making rhubarb and dandelion wine, bottle by bottle, in their Minnesota basement– now produce over 15,000 cases annually of traditional grape wines. Their operation has grown to include a 20-acre vineyard, tasting room, gift shop, wedding facilities and picnic area.

The grounds are expansive and charming and look like a scene taken from a page out of *Home and Garden Magazine*. Potted flowerbeds, fashioned from aged wine barrels and brimming with colorful wild-flowers, are positioned throughout the courtyard. Rose gardens hug a rustic wooden fence, and a splendid 24-foot gazebo offers views of the creek, for which the winery was named. Stroll across the footbridge to the shaded, grassy lawn and pass away the time while listening to the jazz music and enjoying a glass of wine.

WINE LIST

Chardonnay

White Cabernet Sauvignon

Green Hungarian
"Old Vine" Grenache

Sangiovese

Petite Syrah

Double Dog Red
"Old Vine" Zinfandel

Duet **(Late harvest**
Cabernet Zinfandel blend)

Decadencia Chocolate Port

CHAMPAGNE LIST

Grand Cuvee Champagne
Almond Champagne

MUST TASTE

White Cabernet Sauvignon
Almond Champagne

EVENTS

Wilson Creek's lively atmosphere and events have earned it a reputation as "the popular and fun winery". Throughout the year, the family hosts celebrations like sunset jazz, symphony and pop concerts, a harvest party grape stomp, and Mother's Day brunch. They also specialize in weddings, banquets, and large parties.

Through the years many of the famous sayings and poems about wine have rarely been taken seriously, but the Falkners embrace their wonders. Their interest in wine became a passion once they decided, as a young couple, that they wanted to build a winery in Temecula. Today the Falkner Winery is well known. They have two sincere desires: to develop a great and famous selection of wines, and to create an atmosphere in and around their winery that will persuade others to join in their passionate love of the grape.

Their redwood winery sits 1,500 feet above Rancho California Road, and offers top-of-the-hill views from a shady terrace, where a leafy green canopy frames a view of impeccably tended vines and lofty mountains.

Falkner

Winery

65

The Falkner Winery draws many different visitors who appreciate its sophisticated yet relaxed ambiance. They take pleasure from the quality of the Mediterranean and Tuscan style wines. Many take advantage of Falkner's wine appreciation classes, in order to learn about the differences in flavor, bouquet and texture among various kinds of wines – some, which explode with butteriness or reverberate with peppery spice. These lessons are usually informal and resemble the kind of parties where the guests congregate in the kitchen and discuss wine.

Sunday afternoons from 1:00 p.m. to 3:00 p.m. (Spring through Fall) enjoy wine tasting at the outdoor bar while listening to live complimentary jazz concerts. Then browse the art gallery, and catch up with friends during an afternoon alfresco picnic in the winery's beautiful garden setting.

WINE LIST

Sauvignon Blanc
Fumé Blanc
Chardonnay
Viognier
Riesling
Rosato
Cello
Amante
Syrah
Merlot
Cabernet Sauvignon
Meritage

MUST TASTE

Amante

EVENTS

Falkner Winery's attractive outdoor setting lends itself beautifully to wedding ceremonies and receptions, as well as complimentary jazz concerts performed on Sunday afternoons, spring through fall. The winery also features wine tasting classes and private and group tours.

Longshadow Ranch is quite possibly one of the most picturesque wineries in Temecula. Situated just off the main road on Calle Contento, this winery combines the charms of the country with the old west influence of Temecula's past.

The lush rural setting and western storefront design of the tasting room almost instantly brings to mind a scene out of some marvelous western movie. Here, guests can relax on a wooden porch, or enjoy a bottle of estate wine while touring the vineyards in a horse drawn carriage or on a hayride.

LONGSHADOW RANCH

The ranch is the inspiration of the owner, John Brodersen. Born and raised in Wyoming, John would spend most of his days riding horses under the blue expansive sky. By the time he was married, John and his wife were living on a boat in the Dana Point Harbor. They enjoyed their home and surroundings, but wanted to have children and desired to give them the type of life that had made their own childhood so memorable – farming and riding horses. After considerable thought, they decided to move to Temecula. Here, their children could run horses, work in the vineyard, and experience the same childhood pleasures as they had once enjoyed.

Today, the Brodersens' extend this life to their guests. Even if it's only for a few hours, visitors at this winery can enjoy the adventure and the romance of a ranch with horses, wide-open spaces, blue sky and wine.

WINE LIST

White Grenache
Sangiovese
Reata Red **(blend of Merlot, Cabernet Sauvignon, Syrah and Cabernet Franc)**
Ponderosa Port

MUST TASTE

White Grenache

MOUNT PALOMAR VINEYARDS

Mount Palomar Vineyard and Winery stands in secluded splendor on the brow of a steep hill, presenting visitors with one of the best views of the Temecula Valley.

From the hilltop picnic area, as far as the eye can see, stretches a broad vale of green vines intersected at intervals by snug farms and square-topped estates all framed by 360 degrees of high mountains.

It is not only Mount Palomar's view that is impressive, one sip of their wines immediately reveals the owner's passion for creating exceptional and unique wines. As with many fine vineyards, Mount Palomar cultivates the varieties of grapes best suited for their warm Mediterranean climate and soil.

& WINERY

In 1989, they grafted their 20-year old vines to the Tuscan variety of Sangiovese – the first of any Italian variety to be planted in this region. Now, less than a decade later, their Sangiovese is winning numerous awards. The vineyard has also expanded their market to include not only the classic California wines under their label, but also Mediterranean type wines produced under the Rey Sol name, as well as other traditional Italian wines under the Castelletto label.

We suggest that you make this your final stop along the Temecula wine tasting tour. Pick up a bottle of estate wine and a sandwich at the winery's Mediterranean deli, and enjoy watching the sun as it sinks below the horizon, turning your view into an airbrushed painting of pink and orange sky set against the enormous mountainous silhouette.

WINE LIST

Cortese
Chardonnay
Sangiovese
Trovato
Meritage
Syrah
Shorty's Bistro Red
Temecula Rosé
Riesling
Cream Sherry
Limited Reserve Port

MUST TASTE

Cortese

EVENTS

Mount Palomar offers an exciting array of annual events. Every weekend guests can enjoy touring the cellar and library while tasting unreleased and pre-released wines directly from the barrel. The winery also features a candlelight Valentine's dinner, Winemaker dinner and Winter Holiday candlelight barrel tasting with progressive dinner.

Miramonte

I magine beginning each morning with a cup of freshly brewed coffee immediately followed by a walk through rolling vineyards. The only sound is the rustling of vines, the beating of a hummingbird's wings, and the distant call of a red-tail hawk. Now picture that each day ends at twilight with a glass of Sangiovese and a stroll through the fields as the setting sun turns grapes into brilliantly colored jewels.

This is how Cane Vanderhoof, one of the owners of Miramonte Winery, begins and ends each day. He describes it as "pure serenity" and strives to create an ambiance that imparts this feeling to his guests.

Winery

Miramonte Winery is the realization of Cane Vanderhoof, a University of California, Berkeley graduate and Bay Area transplant who began working in the wine business by etching keepsake bottles. Ultimately, he wanted to offer his clients a higher quality of wine, so he decided to open an estate in the Temecula Valley.

The wine, location, and ambiance make this estate a favorite among many local residents and tourists. Situated atop a steep hill, the winery features expansive valley views, which showcase the beauty of the region. Come to visit on Friday evenings and enjoy "Flamenco Fridays" where hip swiveling flamenco music is combined with culinary delights and wines which suit every taste. This has become a tradition for many Temecula locals and visitors, and is a wonderful way to make new friends and catch up with old ones.

WINE LIST

Chardonnay
Rhapsody- White Wine Blend
Sauvignon Blanc
Syrah
Cinsault Rose
Rhapsody –Red Wine Blend
Sangiovese

CHAMPAGNE LIST

Brut Champagne
Blanc de Noirs Champagne

MUST TASTE

Opulente

EVENTS

Miramonte Winery features exceptional events to complement their exceptional wines. One such event is Cinema Classics where guests view classic films on the big screen. The winery also offers wine tasting classes where students compare Temecula wines with those from other well-known wine regions. Finally, be sure to visit during the ever-popular Flamenco Fridays, where guests enjoy live flamenco music and wine.

Driving through the beautiful rolling hills, citrus groves and lush vineyards of the Temecula Valley, visitors come upon, quite unexpectedly, a medieval fortress. Baily Vineyard and Winery is an astonishing reproduction of a European fortress with ivy-covered walls, and knights in shining armor. Along with these obvious Medieval surroundings are gargoyles, archways and a pavilion of columns leading to a European inspired tasting room and restaurant.

At the restaurant, guests may choose to dine inside at Bacchus Hall or outdoors on the lovely garden terrace. The cuisine is officially Californian and features meals as simple as a burger and fries or as delectable as a charbroiled Salmon Filet. Many of the selections are prepared with ingredients picked that morning from the winery's vegetable-herb garden.

BAILY VINEYARDS & WINERY

The Baily's story begins in Germany, where Phil served in the United States military. It was there that they were first introduced to wine and almost instantly became enchanted. They celebrated their first wedding anniversary in the Napa Valley, and as Carol Baily describes it, "their love for wine and each other grew." In 1981, they bought a small home in the Temecula Valley Wine Country, high on a hill, away from the main road. They planted one acre of vines to make wine for friends and family. In no time, they met local winemakers, John Moramarco of Callaway Coastal Vineyards, the Cilurzos, and Doc Filsinger - all of whom encouraged them to open their own winery. On the faith and motivation of their new

friends, Phil and Carol Baily along with their two sons Chris and Pat, planted 'Mother's Vineyard' on Mother's Day, 1982. Four years later they opened a small tasting room with one nouveau wine. After three years, they outgrew their small tasting room and founded Baily Winery at its present location where Phil Baily, having found his métier, has continued to create additional wines that have garnered much attention and many awards.

WINE LIST

Chardonnay
Montage
Riesling
TV White
Rosé of Cabernet Sauvignon
Muscat Blanc
TV Red **(Sangiovese)**
Merlot
Cabernet Sauvignon
Meritage
Serenity **(Late Harvest Chardonnay)**

Callaway Coastal Vineyard

Temecula's largest and best known winery is Callaway Coastal. Situated on a bluff high above Rancho California Road, the great picture windows of Callaway Coastal add to the pleasure of wine tasting in the Temecula Valley. Seven hundred and sixty acres of rolling vineyards combine the charms of the ancient and famous vineyards of Bourgogne and Bordeaux with the benefit of being within easy driving distance from most of Southern California.

Many visitors choose Callaway Coastal as their first stop in Temecula Wine Country. The grand entrance, bedecked with California poppies and African daisies, is lure enough, but that is often surpassed by the winery's flavorful fruit forward wines and its many amenities. Callaway Coastal features complimentary estate tours -where visitors learn the ins and outs of wine production- as well as a gourmet restaurant located directly opposite the great doors of the winery.

& Winery

85

The food is excellent and the picturesque setting welcomes visitors with lovely vistas of miles of green vineyards backdropped by jagged mountains.

One of the most impressive features of Callaway Coastal is their commitment to conservation. They employ several natural and non-invasive methods to restrict the pests and weeds that are known to damage grapevines. Indigeneous grasses, which provide a habitat for predatory insects that eat the harmful pests, are now encouraged to grow amid the vines thus reducing the need for pesticides. Chemical weed killers have been replaced by mechanical weeding. And tall perches are positioned throughout the grounds for predatory red-tailed hawks and owls to keep watch over the field. It's encouraging to know that Callaway Coastal is leading the area in ecological conservation, and all the while continuing to create exceptional wines.

CALLAWAY
Coastal

WINE LIST

Pinot Gris
Viognier
Chardonnay
Sauvignon Blanc
Nebbiolo Bello
Dolcetto
Merlot
Syrah
Muscat Canelli
Roussanne
Meritage
Zinfandel
Cabernet Sauvignon

MUST TASTE

Coastal Reserve Syrah

EVENTS

Given that Calloway Coastal is the largest winery in Temecula, it is only fitting that they have many spectacular events. Public and private tours are given daily. There are wedding and banquet facilities, wine and cheese pairing classes, winemaker dinners, sensory perception wine tasting classes, and 'must experience' winter holiday and Valentine candlelight dinners.

J oe and Nancy Hart of Hart Winery are an inspiration to those who have ever dreamed of owning and operating a winery, but have given up too soon at the specter of high expense. The Harts started out as schoolteachers (Nancy still teaches) working in Carlsbad in nearby San Diego County. Passionate about wine, Joe wanted to buy land to plant a vineyard and construct a winery. In 1970, they discovered the Temecula Valley and after much research deemed Temecula Wine Country to be ideal. In 1973, they took the first step in pursuing Joe's dream and purchased twelve acres. They began planting almost immediately, and within six years had their first crush.

HART WINERY

The initial vintages of Hart wine were produced on a very limited budget with only two wine tanks, a dozen oak barrels, and a crusher they ran by hand – since they didn't yet have electricity. That first year they made 120 cases, carefully hand filling and labeling each bottle. Since then, Joe Hart has gone on to craft fifteen different varietals and production is currently at 5,000 cases per year. After twenty-three harvests, Joe still loves what he does. It's encouraging to see the sense of accomplishment, and love for wine that he continues to have.

From its earliest days, Hart has had a strong commitment to creating quality wines. The winery traditionally turns out dry varietals, which are best enjoyed with food and lend themselves well to steak dinners, fish, and hearty barbeques.

While other wineries may have a larger more elaborate tasting facility, Hart's rustic barn-style tasting room, with its long, narrow porch and red-wood paneling fits in beautifully within Temecula's wine country setting.

Inside, a very tiny tasting room houses French and American oak barrels stacked one on top of the other and contributes to the overall enjoyable ambiance.

WINE LIST

Estate Fumé Blanc
Estate Viognier
Grenache Rosé
Sangiovese
Barbera
Tempranillo
Old Vine Zinfandel
Grenache-Syrah
Syrah
Estate Merlot
Stonelake Vineyard Merlot

MUST TASTE

Syrah

Temecula Valley Highlights

Every spring, Temecula's deep blue skies erupt in a riot of multicolored hot-air balloons during the Temecula Valley Balloon and Wine Festival. The thousands of visitors who attend participate in a springtime tradition that's as integral to Temecula life as its wines.

Located at Lake Skinner Regional Park, the festival gets underway Friday evening with a "Balloon Glow", where tethered hot air balloons become illuminated against the night sky and appear to dance in synchronized fashion – all to the beat of lively music. The real talent lies with the pilots who ignite and extinguish the balloons' burners to achieve this effect.

The following morning, the gates open at 6:00 a.m. and the colorful crafts take to the sky by 7:00 a.m. (weather permitting). It's an awesome sight as the sun peaks over the horizon and dances in the tops of the trees, and over fifty brilliantly colored balloons sail over the lake.

From the air, the view is even more spectacular. Passengers glide over Southern California's wine country and are rewarded with panoramic views of rolling vineyards, grand estates and scenic mountains ranges. It's best to reserve tickets a few months in advance if you are interested in enjoying a balloon ride during the festival. For those who would like to experience flying on a smaller scale, complimentary tethered hot air balloon rides are also available.

If you would just as soon keep your feet on the ground and something warm in your belly, make your way to the festival's gourmet food and wine garden. Here adults can enjoy tasting gourmet cheeses, hors d'oeuvres, specialty food, and world-class wines produced in the Temecula Wine County.

In addition to hot air ballooning and wine tasting, the festival also includes live entertainment with top-name bands, an art and craft fair, and a kids science discovery center – featuring hands-on exhibits and performances geared toward science and education.

The festival is usually held in June, but it is best to contact the Temecula Valley Balloon and Wine Festival Association for specific dates and details surrounding the fête. Call 909/676-6713, or visit the web site at www.tvbwf.com.

The famous arched sign over Temecula's main street commemorates the town's early days of rancheros and vaqueros – when steer wrestling, team roping, and bronco riding were all part of a day's work, and managing herds of cattle meant riding in the saddle from dawn to dusk. Today, Temecula's Frontier Days Rodeo, held every year over Memorial Day Weekend, celebrates this era with rough-and-tumble demonstrations and challenging competitions.

Temecula's Professional Cowboys Rodeo Association-sanctioned rodeo features some of the nation's top cowboys, who are just as rough and ready as any from the past. In the American wild-west spirit of competition, these riders take off at breakneck speeds roping calves, wrestling steer, team roping, bareback riding, barrel racing and bronco riding.

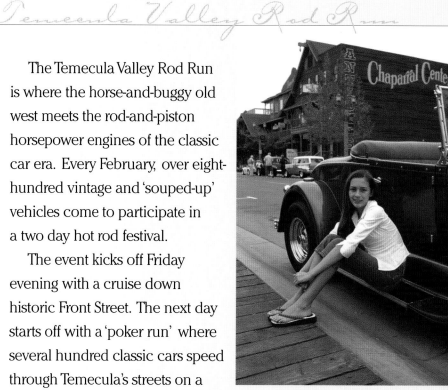

The Temecula Valley Rod Run is where the horse-and-buggy old west meets the rod-and-piston horsepower engines of the classic car era. Every February, over eight-hundred vintage and 'souped-up' vehicles come to participate in a two day hot rod festival.

The event kicks off Friday evening with a cruise down historic Front Street. The next day starts off with a 'poker run' where several hundred classic cars speed through Temecula's streets on a scavenger hunt. The lead-footed drivers race to seven different locations, stopping only to pick up one playing card. At the finish line whoever has the best hand wins the title and three-hundred dollars. Sunday, the owners park their cars along Old Town Front Street for visitors to get a closer look.

Wine, of course, is Temecula's greatest treasure. However, for those who would like to combine a relaxing day in the country with the energy and excitement of city life- Las Vegas style, travel beyond the sweet perfume of the Valley's vineyards and orchards to Pechanga Resort & Casino, Temecula's premier gaming palace.

The resort blends the grandeur and entertainment of a Las Vegas-style casino with the luxury and comfort of a full

service resort. Conveniently situated off Interstate 15 on Pechanga Parkway, the hotel features 522 beautifully appointed rooms – many of which offer sweeping views of the valley, an 88,800 square foot casino with 2,000 state-of-the-art slot machines, a high stakes Bingo Hall and 63 table games including Blackjack, Pai Gow, Let It Ride, 3-Card Poker, and Mini-Baccarat, as well as seven restaurants, four lounges, live entertainment, pool, spa, health club and meeting and convention accommodations.

After a full day in the casino there is nothing more relaxing than lounging poolside in the California sunshine, sipping a cool drink and dreaming of Lady Luck, nothing except, perhaps enjoying a massage at the hotel spa. Afterwards, visitors can treat themselves to a fine meal at any one of the hotel's gourmet restaurants – The Great Oak Steakhouse, Paisano's Italian Restaurant, or The Grotto seafood restaurant – before setting off to enjoy a concert, the theatre or a championship professional boxing match in the hotel's grand ballroom. Finish off the day at the rooftop Eagle's Nest lounge, an intimate bar with an outdoor patio showcasing views of the valley and snowcapped mountains.

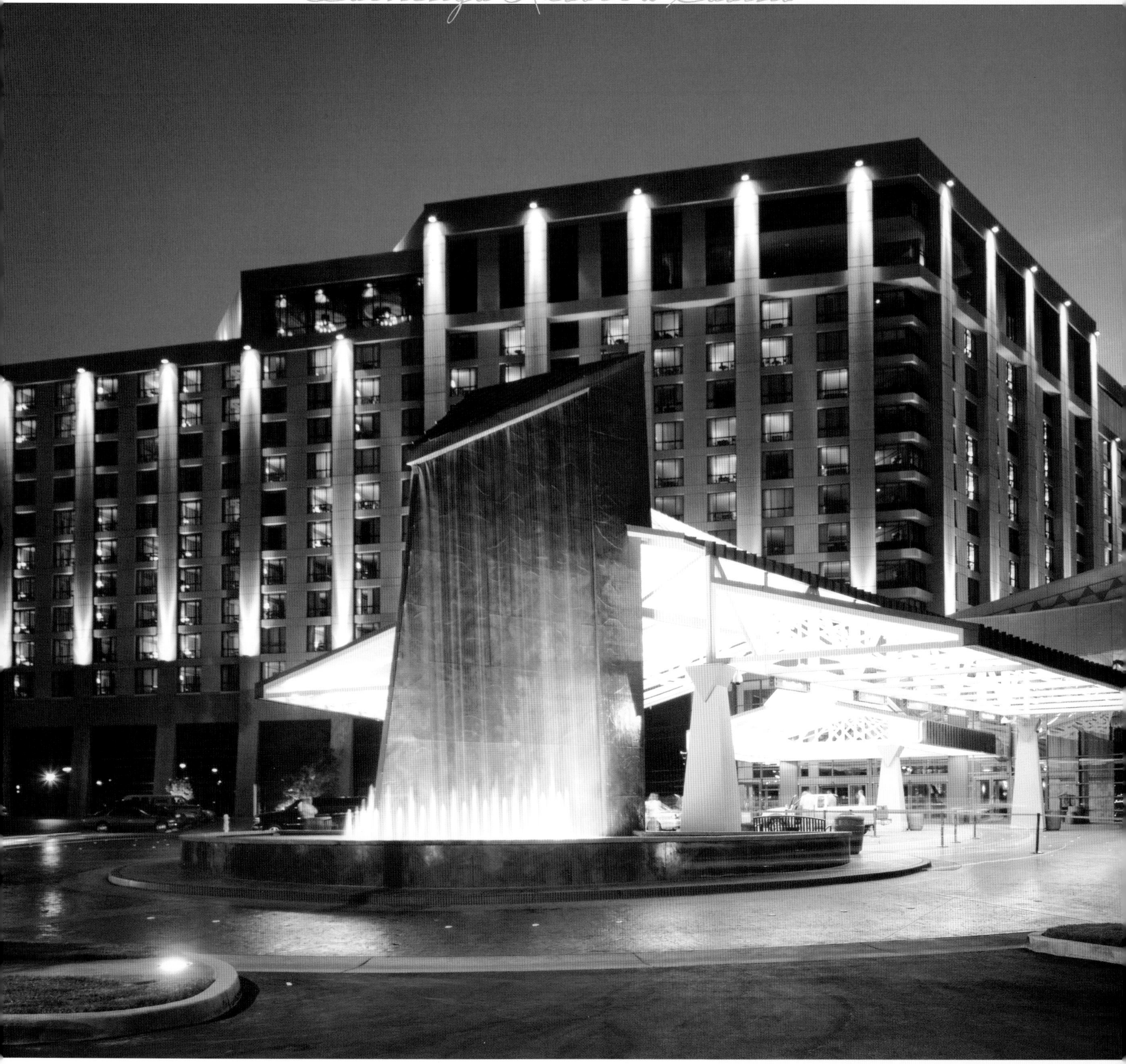

Redhawk Golf Club and Temecula Hills, both managed by CSC Golf Management and PGA Professionals, are two of Temecula's most memorable golf courses.

Redhawk Golf Club, the proud recipient of the coveted four star "Must Play" designation by Golf Digest offers players a spectacular golf experience. Named seventh in the state of California for fine public facilities, this course offers grand views and a peaceful playing environment.

Temeku Hills, nestled in the hills of the Temecula Valley, offers a total golf experience for all skill levels from tournament players to weekend golfers and beginners. Renowned golf course architect Perry Dye has freshly updated Ted Robinson's original design. Golfers will enjoy the beautiful mountain setting with tiered greens, strategically placed bunkers and lakes, and a challenging variety of rolling fairways.

After a round of golf visit the golf shop, grab a bite to eat in the restaurant, or recap the round on the course's 19th hole.

Temecula Valley Golf Courses

REDHAWK GOLF CLUB

45100 Rehawk Parkway
Temecula, California
Telephone: (909) 302-3850
Web: www.redhawkgolfcourse.com

Set in the midst of the Temecula Wine Country, Redhawk Golf Club is beautiful, offering golfers unobstructed views of the Temecula Valley and snow capped peaks of San Bernardino and San Jacinto mountains. The course is the recipient of the coveted "Four Star" rating by Golf Digest Magazine and has been named seventh in the state of California for fine public facilities. The tranquil and diverse playing environment and design has been known to inspire awe from players of all talents.

TEMEKU HILLS GOLF COURSE

41687 Temeku Drive
Temecula, California 92591
Telephone: (909) 694-9998
Web: www.temekuhills.com

Temeku Hills

Temeku Hills Golf and Country Club is one of Temecula's premier golfing facilities. Golfers will enjoy the course's rolling topography, lakes, doglegs, and beautiful challenging greens. Amenities include a 40,000 square foot clubhouse, grass driving range, full service golf shop, banquet room and Grill Room. Come see why Temeku Hills Golf and Country Club is the most popular stop for golfers when visiting the Temecula Valley.

CALIFORNIA DREAMIN'

Telephone: (800) 373-3359
E-mail: David@californiadreamin.com
Web: www.californiadreamin.com

Enjoy a Hot Air Balloon or open cockpit biplane flight over Temecula's beautiful Wine Country. During sunrise, when the sun ascends over the mountain ranges illuminating the valley, the view is spectacular. Upon landing, you will be served a Continental Breakfast including locally crafted champagne, orange juice, coffee and gourmet pastries. A flight certificate and photograph will be awarded to commemorate your flight on California Dreamin' Hot air balloon adventure or biplane flight.

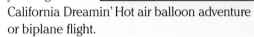

A GRAPE ESCAPE BALLOON ADVENTURE

40335 Winchester Road, Suite E
PMB 226 Temecula, California 92591
Telephone: (800) 965-2122
Web: www.agrapeescape.com

Your escape awaits you over the beautiful Temecula Valley wine country. Experience peace and serenity while drifting over the vineyards as the sun rises over the San Jacinto Mountains. Your flight begins with the inflation of the gentle giant then sixty to seventy-five minutes in the air floating over vineyards, citrus groves and estate homes. Upon landing, enjoy chilled champagne, orange juice and a continental breakfast served picnic style.

THE GRAPELINE WINE COUNTRY SHUTTLE

Telephone: (909) 693-LINE
E-mail: David@californiadreamin.com
Web: www.gogrape.com

Wine taste, picnic, and mingle with friends while the Grapeline Wine Country Shuttle brings you to Temecula's finest wineries and estates. Choose from the convenient weekend shuttle, which provides all-day transportation from most Temecula hotels to the wineries. Or select the Cabernet Tour, which features wine tasting followed by a gourmet picnic lunch in a beautiful garden setting at one of the wineries.

EMBASSY SUITES HOTEL TEMECULA VALLEY WINE COUNTY

29345 Rancho California Road
Temecula, California 92591
Telephone: (909) 676-5656
Web: www.embassysuites.com

The Embassy Suites Temecula Valley Wine Country is an ideal retreat for both business and leisure trips. The beautifully designed hotel combines the comforts of an all suite hotel with the convenience of being centrally located to Temecula's historic Old Town and beautiful wine country. The hotel features a restaurant, swimming pool, hot tub and conference rooms.

The suites have one king size or two double beds, a separate living room with sofa bed, a well-lit dining or work table and

EMBASSY SUITES HOTEL ®

in-room movies. Moreover, all reservations come with a full cooked-to-order breakfast and evening Manager Reception.

INN AT CHURON WINERY

33233 Rancho California Road
Temecula, California 92591
Telephone: (909) 694-9070
Web: www.inatchuronwinery.com

The Inn at Churon Winery is a stunning French Style Chateau located in the heart of Temecula Wine Country. Sixteen beautiful rooms and six elegant suites all feature gas burning fireplaces, Jacuzzi bathtubs for two, a king or double queen size bed and a private balcony  showcasing views of the estate's lovely vineyards. The inn features a winery, wine tasting room, deli, gift shop, conference room and a special event garden ideal for weddings.

LOMA VISTA BED & BREAKFAST

33350 La Serena Way
Temecula, California 92591
Telehone: (909) 676-7047

Loma Vista Bed & Breakfast is a beautiful Mission Style home with panoramic views of the Temecula Valley. Situated high on a hill overlooking Baily Vineyards and Winery, guests can relax on a panoramic patio and enjoy complimentary wine and cheese served in the evening. Ten guest rooms combine the peace and serenity of the Temecula Valley with delightfully decorated rooms, some of which feature morning views of hot air balloons, others that open up to a private courtyard, one with a fireplace and some with Jacuzzi tubs.

 All rooms are air-conditioned and have private bath and showers and include a fullChampagne Breakfast.

PECHANGA RESORT AND CASINO

45000 Pechanga Parkway
Temecula, California 92592
Telephone: (909) 693-1819
Reservations: (888) 732-4264
Web: www.pechanga.com

Conveniently located off Interstate-15 in beautiful wine-country Temecula, Pechanga Resort and Casino has earned the AAA Four Diamond Award and lays claim to the title "California's Best Resort and Casino." Guests can enjoy 24-hour gaming excitement, 522 luxurious rooms and suites, seven exceptional restaurants, top-name entertainment, pool, health club facilities and more. Find out foryourself all this Inland Empire Resort and Casino has to offer.

ALLIE'S AT CALLAWAY

32720 Rancho California Road
Temecula, California 92591
Telephone: 909-694-0560
Web: www.Alliesatcallaway.com

Whether enjoying a light lunch, a glass of wine with our award winning appetizers, or a five-course dinner with wines to compliment each course, your experience at Allie's will be memorable. Allie's at Callaway takes great pride in offering our guests a comfortable & relaxed dining experience like no other. Set atop the vineyards of Callaway Coastal Vineyard & Winery guests enjoy alfresco dining with one of the most creative menus in the valley. Offering fusion cuisine of the Mediterranean and California, Allies combines passionate flavors perfectly married with the freshness of the area. Open for Lunch Monday – Saturday 11:00 a.m. – 3:00 p.m., Champagne Sunday Brunch 11:00 a.m. – 3:00 p.m. and dinner Friday & Saturday 5;00 p.m. – 9:00 p.m. Private Parties available Sunday through Thursday evening.

BAILY'S

Owners Chris and Kim Baily have put together one of Temecula's finest restaurant. In operation since 1992 and due to relocate to Old Town Temecula late fallof 2003, Baily's has become famous for dishes such as Salmon Wellington, Tequila Shrimp Flambé, Chicken Schnitzel and fine steaks and exquisite

daily fish specials. The menu at Baily's changes weekly to showcase the skills of Chef David Wells and his culinary staff. If you are in the mood for fine food and professional service in an elegant setting, I highly recommend Baily's.

CAROL'S RESTAURANT AT BAILY WINERY

33440 La Serena Way
Temecula, California 92591
Telephone: (909) 676-9243
Web: www.bailywinery.com

Weather touring wine country or simply looking for a good restaurant, Carol's located at Baily Winery is an excellent choice. Guests can select to dine inside Bacchus Hall where gargoyles, knights, and an enormous fireplace add a Medieval flavor, or alfresco on the pergola covered terrace next to the Cabernet Sauvignon vines. Open for lunch Tuesday thru Sunday, Carol's features a selection of salads, sandwiches, and entrees such as grilled fresh fish, steak, and pasta dishes. To accompany your meal Carol's offers an extensive beer and wine list featuring Baily and other Temecula Valley and domestic wines.

THE SMOKEHOUSE CAFE AT PONTE FAMILY ESTATE WINERY

35053 Rancho California Road
Temecula, California 92591
Telephone: (909) 694-8855
Serving Mediterranean fare
E-mail: msmith@pontewinery.com
Web: www.pontewinery.com

Enjoy your day in the country with casual patio dining adjacent to the vineyards. The Smokehouse Café, located at Ponte Family Estate Winery, blends the influences of the local vineyards and farmers' markets with the tastes of Ponte wines, to create a delightfully unique version of California Cooking. Highlighted by a wood-burning pizza oven preparing signature California pizzas, country-inspired sandwiches, Saint-Louise Style Ribs, house created salads, Ponte wine by the glass, and micro-brew draft beer. Dine on the

veranda, and enjoy these delicious creations while taking in the breathtaking views of the surrounding mountains.

BAILY VINEYARD & WINERY

33440 La Serena
Temecula, California 92591
Telephone: (909) 676-9463
Winery Hours: 10:00 a.m.- 5:00 p.m.

CALLAWAY COASTAL VINEYARD & WINERY

32720 Rancho California Road
Temecula California 92591
Telephone: (800) 472-2377
Web: www.callawaycoastal.com
Winery Hours: 10:30 a.m.- 5:00 p.m.

CHURON WINERY

33233 Rancho California Road
Temecula, California 92591
Telephone: (909) 694-9071
Web: www.innatchuronwinery.com
Winery Hours: 10:30 a.m. – 5:30 p.m.

CILURZO VINEYARD & WINERY

41220 Calle Contento
Temecula, California 92591
Telephone: (909) 676-5250
Web: wwwcilurzowine.com
Winery Hours: 10:00 a.m.- 5:00 p.m.

FALKNER WINERY

40620 Calle Contento
Temecula, California 92591
Telephone: (909) 676-8231
Web: www.falknerwinery.com
Winery Hours: 10:00 a.m. – 5:00 p.m.

FILSINGER VINEYARDS & WINERY

39050 De Portola Road
Temecula, California 92591
Telephone: (909) 302-6363
Winery Hours: Friday 11:00 a.m. – 4:00
p.m. Weekends 10:00 a.m. – 5:00 p.m.

HART WINERY

41300 Avenida Biona
Temecula, California 92591
Telephone: (909) 676-6300
Winery Hours: 9:00 a.m. - 4:30 p.m.

LONGSHADOW RANCH VINEYARDS & WINERY

39847 Calle Contento
Temecula, California 92591
Telephone: (909) 587-6221
Web: www.longshadowranch.net
Winery Hours:
Weekends 10:00 a.m. – 5:00 a.m.

KEYWAYS VINEYARD & WINERY

37338 De Portola Road
Temecula, California 92591
Telephone: (909) 302-7888
Web: www.keywayswinery.com
Winery Hours: 10:00 a.m. – 5:00 p.m.

MAURICE CARRIE WINERY

34225 Rancho California Road
Temecula, California 92591
Telephone: (909) 676-1711
Winery Hours: 10:00 a.m.- 5:00 p.m.

MIRAMONTE WINERY

33410 Rancho California Road
Temecula, California 92591
Telephone: (909) 506-5500
Web: www.celebrationcellars.com
Winery Hours: 10:00 a.m. – 5:00 p.m.

MOUNT PALOMAR WINERY

33820 Rancho California Road
Temecula, California 92591
Telephone: (909) 676-5047
Web: www.mountpalomar.com
Winery Hours: 10:00 a.m. – 4:45 p.m.

PALUMBO FAMILY VINEYARDS & WINERY

40150 Barksdale Circle
Temecula, California 92591
Telephone: (909) 676-7900
Web: www.palumbofamilyvineyards.com
Winery Hours:
Weekends 10:00 a.m. – 5:00 p.m.

PONTE FAMILY ESTATE WINERY

35053 Rancho California Road
Temecula CA 92592
Telephone: (909)694-8855
Web: www.pontewinery.com
Winery Hours: 10:00 a.m. – 5:00 p.m.

STUART CELLARS

33515 Rancho California Road
Temecula, California 92591
Telephone: (909) 676-6414
Web: www.stuartcellars.com
Winery Hours: 10:00 – 5:00 p.m.

TEMECULA SPRINGS RESORT AND SOUTH COAST WINERY

34843 Rancho California Road
Temecula CA 92591
Telephone: (909) 587-9463
Web: www.southcoastwinery.com
Opening in 2003

THORNTON WINERY

32575 Rancho California Road
Temecula, California 92591
Telephone: (909) 699-0099
Web: www.thorntonwine.com
Winery Hours: 11:00 a.m. – 5:00 p.m.

VAN ROEKEL VINEYARDS AND WINERY

34567 Rancho California Road
Temecula, California 92591
Telephone: (909) 699-6961
Winery Hours: 10:00 a.m. – 5:00 p.m.

WILSON CREEK WINERY AND VINEYARD

35960 Rancho California Road
Temecula, California 92591
Telephone: (909) 699-9463
Web: www.wilsoncreekwinery.com
Winery Hours: 10:00 a.m. – 5:00 p.m.

Order Form

SHIP TO:

Name

Address

City

State   Zip

Telephone

E-mail

Quantity	Book Price	Shipping & Handling	Subtotal
	$27.50	$5.00	
California residents please add sales tax of $2.13 per book.			
		Total	

Please send check or money order to:
Vista Pacifica Publishing Company
P.O. Box 373
Dana Point, CA 92629-0373

Telephone: (949) 395-2878
E-mail: Vistapacifica@usa.com
Web site: www.vistapacificapublishing.com

VISTA PACIFICA PUBLISHING COMPANY
Dana Point, California

Wine Tasting

REDEEMABLE FOR ONE COMPLIMENTARY

TEMECULA WINE COUNTRY

Compliments of Vista Pacifica Publishing Company and participating Temecula wineries. This certificate is redeemable for one complimentary wine tasting at any one of the wineries included in this book, except Thornton Winery, when the bearer buys the first wine tasting at the regular price. Please see reverse side for valid requirements and restrictions.

Void if electronically copied, scanned, or altered.

Please remove gift certificates along perforated score.

Redeemable for One Complimentary Wine Tasting Tour

THE GRAPELINE WINE COUNTRY SHUTTLE

Redeemable for one complimentary wine tasting tour on The Grapeline Wine Country Shuttle when the bearer buys the first wine tasting tour at the regular price. Compliments of Vista Pacifica Publishing Company and The Grapeline Wine Country Shuttle. Please see reverse side for valid requirements and restrictions.

Void if electronically copied, scanned, or altered.

TEMECULA WINE COUNTRY

This section should be completed by the winery when the certificate is redeemed.
Mail completed certificate to: Vista Pacifica Publishing Company · PO Box 373 · Dana Point, CA 92629-0373

Guest Name

Guest Home Address

Guest City   State   Zip

Guest home telephone number

Winery

Signature of Winery Employee

Certificate is good for one complimentary wine tasting with the purchases of one wine tasting at the regular price. Offer not valid at all times. Restrictions apply. Vista Pacifica Publishing Company is not responsible for any changes in individual winery operation or policy. By use of this certificate, consumer agrees to release Vista Pacifica Publishing Company from any liability in connection with their travel to and visit at any participating Temecula wineries. This certificate may not be reproduced and cannot be used in conjunction with any other promotional offers. Certificate must be redeemed at participating wineries by December 31, 2005. Void where prohibited. Void if electronically copied, scanned or altered. Certificate expires December 31, 2005.

THE GRAPELINE WINE COUNTRY SHUTTLE

This section should be completed by The Grapeline Wine Country Shuttle when the certificate is redeemed.
Mail completed certificate to: Vista Pacifica Publishing Company · PO Box 373 · Dana Point, CA 92629-0373

Name of Guest

Guest Home Address

Guest City   State   Zip

Guest Home Telephone Number

Signature

Certificate is good for one complimentary wine tasting tour with the purchase of one wine tasting tour at the regular price. Offer valid Sunday through Thursday. Subject to availability. Advanced reservations recommended. Restrictions apply. Vista Pacifica Publishing Company is not responsible for any changes in individual tour operation or policy. By use of this certificate, consumer agrees to release Vista Pacifica Publishing Company from any liability in connection with their travel to and visit of Temecula while on The Grapeline Wine Country Shuttle. This certificate may not be reproduced and cannot be used in conjunction with any other promotional offers. Certificate must be redeemed at The Grapeline Wine Country Shuttle by December 31, 2005. Void where prohibited. Void if electronically copied, scanned or altered. Certificate expires December 31, 2005.

Please remove gift certificates along perforated score.